PRAISE

MUSIC

D.G. GEIS

PRAISE

MUSIC

GUERNICA
World
EDITIONS
TORONTO · BUFFALO · LANCASTER (U.K.)
2018

Michael Mirolla, editor
Cover design and interior layout: Rafael Chimicatti
Front cover image by Noah Geis
Guernica Editions Inc.
1569 Heritage Way, Oakville, (ON), Canada L6M 2Z7
2250 Military Road, Tonawanda, N.Y. 14150-6000 U.S.A.
www.guernicaeditions.com

Distributors:
University of Toronto Press Distribution,
5201 Dufferin Street, Toronto (ON), Canada M3H 5T8
Gazelle Book Services, White Cross Mills
High Town, Lancaster LA1 4XS U.K.

First edition.
Printed in Canada.

Legal Deposit — Third Quarter
Library of Congress Catalog Card Number: 2018948500
Library and Archives Canada Cataloguing in Publication
Geis, D. G., author
Praise music / D.G. Geis. -- First edition.

(Guernica world editions ; 12)
Poems.
ISBN 978-1-77183-381-3 (softcover)

I. Title. II. Series: Guernica world editions ; 12

PS3607.E3695P73 2018   11'.6   C2018-903711-3

For Robin, mid-flight

Contents

Magic :: 1

Groundwork of the Metaphysics of Morals :: 2

Original Sin :: 4

Mockumentary :: 6

Free Survival Guide :: 7

To the Barmaid at Clifford's Bar and Grill :: 8

Country Funeral :: 10

Visit to a Small Planet :: 12

Marriage :: 14

Heaven :: 16

At the Huguenot Cemetery :: 18

Paradise :: 20

For a Child Dead from a Playground Fall :: 21

The Blessing of the Animals :: 22

Praise Music :: 24

Psalm 152 (A Song of Ascent) :: 25

State of the Universe Address :: 29

Counting Crows :: 30

If Cowboys Were Cancer Cells :: 33

Mad Science :: 35

Cultural Heritage Map :: 37

Job's Children :: 38

The Prodigal :: 40

The History Channel :: 41

Weatherman :: 42

A Seventy-Year-Old Father
    Hikes Through the East Texas Piney Woods
    with His Seven-Year-old Autistic Son :: 43

Tooth Fairy :: 45

Ask Marilyn :: 46

Estate Sale :: 48

Lullaby :: 49

Two Kinds :: 50

Singularity :: 52

Class of '67 :: 53

Cenotaph :: 55

Bandera Family Practice :: 56

A Stockyard Liturgy :: 58

To a Wife Drowned while Drinking :: 59

Tulsa 1959 :: 61

School of Life :: 64

The Dead Can Swing Too :: 66

Acknowledgments :: 67

About the Author :: 68

Magic

This sleight of hand
called life —

the wives
we make disappear

and children
we pull out of hats.

The parents who, over time,
we saw painlessly in half

and the complicated knots
that untie themselves.

The doves and serpents
pulled from Jehovah's empty sleeve

to misdirect
the mischief of our making:

the compassion we feel
for a rag in the road

believing it to be
a squashed puppy.

Or the cock killed for Asclepius
to thank Houdini God,

our Chained Magician
drowning

in his locked box.

Groundwork of the Metaphysics of Morals

For Marc Sheehan

I'm betting on a multiverse
where better versions of me

stretch through eternity
unfolding like paper dolls.

The lesser Greg might be perched
on a bar stool in South Houston

eying the prize
of the pipefitter's estranged wife,

but further downstream,
a greater Greg is walking

his cancer stricken neighbor's *Weimaraner.*
It is a masterpiece of engineering

that all these Gregs exist, *so to speak,*
in the same skin.

And that moral progress is a team sport.
That as my life plays out

like the B side of an old 45,
I could still end up being,

through some inexplicable act
of Divine Hooey, a greatest hit.

And that behind the scenes,
an army of celestial *doppelgangers*

is picking up the slack, filling in gaps,
chained to their oars, rowing like hell,

trying to make a better man of me.

Original Sin

That sly infant has his own ideas.
Look in those eyes —

a pint-sized Svengali
swaddled in possibility.

But behind that beatific smile,
a beast-in-waiting.

Which will torture small animals
and fan secret fires?

Strangle truck stop waitresses
or beat his wife with a 5 iron?

And which will discover
a cure for cancer

and give a genocidal dictator
a new lease on life?

On this, Doctors Freud
and Augustine agree.

God only knows
where the child ends and the lie begins.

But the devil, with his practical paws,
lets us choose.

Whether, in the long run, therapy or drugs
work best for you.

Why the moon looks like a sugar cookie
on this warm November night

and what will come from chasing happiness
when those adorable tiny feet

finally hit the ground.

Mockumentary

Count the leashed dogs
pulling homeowners

down the sidewalk
or the neighborly oaks lining up

to shake hands across the street,
the garbage truck,

stumbling down Del Monte
with all the lives, neatly bagged,

crushed in the back.
And don't forget Mr. Sun,

the bright-eyed prosecutor,
rising to make his case,

the "For Sale" signs
further down the road,

and the mailman
in his light blue uniform,

efficient as always,
delivering this, Dear Resident,

your final offer.

Free Survival Guide

When a day fights back like this
you forget about mankind's shenanigans

or the freeze-dried meals
being hawked on TV.

Your first responder, the mourning dove,
doesn't sing from fear or plan for emergencies,

but from under the eaves,
announces each morning the news of the day:

the sabbath smell of grass,
the sun's chanted sutra

awakening clouds
in their blue cloister.

Or the simple-minded ants
garrisoning the sidewalk.

But even if the world's dogeared pages
were about to close,

what difference would it make?
You would still have the best seat in the house.

And like the first crisp bite of an apple
or the last act of a perfectly staged tragedy,

it would dawn on you — perhaps suddenly,
that no matter how long or loud you clapped,

there would be no encore.
And that whatever the day might bring,

it would still be good.

To the Barmaid at Clifford's Bar and Grill

Crookstown, County Cork

Dear Katy
with the turnstile smile,
perhaps you remember the poet from Texas
whose car blew a tire on R585?
You, a 17-year-old girl working
in your father's bar;
I, the man who could not "keep left" —
the perfect Irish cartoon
of a reckless cowboy.

What can I tell you about my trip to Ireland?
How I ended up in the background
of a 1000 German tourist snapshots.
The sound of roller boards clattering
over cobblestones
and the topknots of god knows
how many Dublin teen agers,
masterless Samurai roaming
the vast shogunate of the Temple Bar.

The farmers that dressed like golfers
and the Japanese schoolchildren
crawling on the statue of Oscar Wilde.
The Viking-helmeted Norsemen
cruising along the Liffey
in WWII landing craft.
Irish burglar alarms
that sound like herders
whistling for their dogs.
And your Garda
rousting drunks,
as solid and implacable
as an English door lock.

The insouciance of cabbies
weaving in and out of bicyclists,
all pedaling furiously
like Mormon missionaries.
Chased by history —
but with God at their back.

(Dear Lord, is there anything sadder
than an Irishman on a bicycle
in a coat and tie?)

O Katy,
you do not have to travel far
to see the world.
It is all laid out before you

Our Lady driving clouds like cattle
across the Cork sky.
The July sun pinned
like an orange corsage to a prom dress.
All that light pureed
into what is durable and green.

But if you must travel, stay at home;
cruise the internet.
read poetry, watch TV
(and leave biography for bedtime).
Remember that everything unravels
in the face of chance
and that all voids lead to home.

Keep to the hearth.
Stay on your side of the bar.
Marry a handsome farm boy.
Spin gold from hay.
Die healthy as an Adventist.

And think of all the people
in this great magical world

saving up for microwaves.

Country Funeral

I never knew you were Baptist.
Nor, I suspect, did you.

Perhaps it was the funeral director
or your most recent ex

that finally got you into church.
Your waterless baptism, surprise testimony

to the suddenness of your saving.
Passing alongside your open casket,

my noncommittal shadow
must have tickled just a bit,

because in that nearly arranged smile,
I thought I saw the candle

of your face still flickering.
In your pressed *Wranglers*

and straw *Resistol*
covering those idle hands,

it looked as if the devil's business
had finally been concluded —

with your honky-tonk soul
starched now for all eternity,

ready for a night out on the town.
And your brother's boy, the cowboy preacher,

comparing Jesus to a rodeo clown
willing to take all the hits,

rolling around in his barrel for days,
waving off that un-rideable bull.

And the pickup trucks on the church lawn,
lined up like celestial stepping stones,

more numerous than the stars
engendering Abraham's children.

With mourners squeezing slowly
down the narrow chute of grass

between sanctuary and Fellowship Hall,
that Dry Valhalla of antique trophy buckles

and green bean casserole,
of aproned angels and third cousins,

all waiting to pour lemonade
in paper cups

and offer their condolences.

Visit to a Small Planet

No telling
what He thinks — *or if.*

His ears,
a zillion-light-years wide,

pressed to the fizzy heart
of the universe,

a hydrogen gas bag
folded in on itself

like table napkins
on the Hindenburg,

an omelet,
or a quantum quesadilla.

What we call spiral galaxies,
He calls soup and sandwiches.

What we call supernovas,
He calls shoe polish.

What we call black holes,
He calls a paycheck.

What we call space,
He calls the barstool.

What we call the Big Bang,
He calls Louise.

It's why the sun's
so hysterical

and the moon
so matter of fact.

But it's also why
stars twinkle —

The Big Guy winking at us,
humming a little tune

to Himself,
while he helps Louise

with her zipper.

Marriage

Montaigne compared it
to a birdcage.

Socrates claimed a bad one
made you a philosopher.

Luther prayed the conjugal rose
would open nightly

and believed the marriage bed
a "school for character."

Luther's paradise
proved too heavenly

for postdiluvians
still clinging to their mattresses

as the waters ebbed.
And did Adam,

the first husband,
know that as he hardened

his resolve
and Eve, the first wife,

spread her legs,
creation also moaned?

Or the wolves that howled
when they received their names

would become the dogs
to wag the tail

end of domesticity;
dogs whose days span further

than most marriages
and whose ignorance

knows nothing
of such bliss —

yet still answer
to their names.

That two humans
thrown together by chance

are called spouses.
Or a flock of ravens,

an unkindness.

Heaven

My theology is fuzzy,
but my hopes are high.

Perhaps I'll see my old dog Biscuit
or chill with a friend or two.

And, wonder of wonders,
my headmistress ex-wife

will finally have
my undivided attention.

I'll find out whether God
has a name stitched on His shirt,

or, as *Undercover Boss*,
mans a register behind the counter.

I'm hoping I'll get credit
for all the times

I walked right up to the edge
and stopped — but who's to say?

Maybe the Old Boy
will just shrug his shoulders and say:

"Your craziness is My craziness."
And call it a day.

I have some questions for Socrates
and even a few for Jesus.

But if everything's wrapped up,
there may be nothing left to talk about.

Down here on Goofball Earth,
it's another story.

Tangoing through the void,
hobnobbing with the stars,

confusion only multiplies.
On this bright and zany planet,

we warm to darkness
like soulful Finns, whose apportioned lot

is to be both happy and suicidal
simultaneously.

And so we bow down.
Not in gratitude or with heavy hearts,

but because in this vast Selfie of a universe,
we see ourselves in You.

Sometimes the dummy, sometimes the ventriloquist,
but made in Your image.

Which is, Dear Lord,
where all the trouble begins.

At the Huguenot Cemetery

For Aidan Mathews

The gate is locked,
the squatters settled now in good dirt,
tended there by shadows
and a flock of Irish trees.

Outside the gate,
a bus stop where commuters
queue for rides to God knows where,
shivering in the wealth of wind

like carriage horses
lined up outside *The Shelbourne*,
blanketed, with collars
and harnesses to help

them pull their weight.
Calm in their helplessness,
they stand unblinking
and indifferent in the face of work.

Strange fruit, Geneva's children —
encircled now by bobbing cranes
raised up on one leg to peck away
at blinkered Dublin.

And the hive of day-glo workers
in their drone bumble bee vests,
here to milk fresh honey from cement.
As if to say, the business of life goes on.

Tired émigrés, quarantined
in some eternal freehold,
wedged between an optician's
and a language school, *sale agreed*,

they nap among the hopscotched stones.
And in their final sliver of certainty,
rest blessedly assured, liveried souls
frozen in that place, surrounded there

by gospel commerce, oblivious to nature,
its manual acts and greening priest-talk,
like dioramas in a natural history museum
trace our blind ascent.

Paradise

It's not much of a garden:
January rain and sheeted ice

stretched over the carcass
of a creaking bed frame.

Cellophane leaves with
nothing to disturb them

but the small tracks
of Dürer's children

breaking the crusted grass
with the extra weight

of two ankle monitors.

For a Child Dead from a Playground Fall

The unpacking of the mind's eye
beside the *Paw Patrol* lunchbox.

Wisecracking tractor,
chatty dump truck.

The *Hot Wheels* idling
at a final pit stop

or raucous cop car
in full pursuit.

In the soul's garage,
some batteries last forever.

The least vibration or slightest nudge,
and even the toys cry out;

an absence to make this presence mean
what *Babar* or *Curious George*

will never have the guts to say.
That grief's unstuffing

can speak a kindergartener's vernacular
with pain more fierce

than any high school mascot.
This world through the glassy eye

of a taxidermist or undertaker—
the thousand-yard stare

of a five-year-old's teddy bear.

The Blessing of the Animals

> "Cannibal Chimp
> Snatches Newborn
> And Eats It!"
> —*Newsweek*, October 17, 2017

Nature's mirror shows St. Francis barefoot,
tonsured, preaching to the birds.

For all the good it did,
they never got the word.

The Ark debouched its creatures two by two.
They fled, they bred, what else were they to do?

The flood of irony Creation could awake
was just a little taste of what

a Better Artist might have made,
a world full cooked and not half-baked.

The labyrinth of human nature,
its noisome twists and turns,

was one twist short
where Uncle Monkey was concerned.

To see the world for what it is
the way our gardening parents never did.

Their story was:
"It dropped, we ate it, then we hid."

Of all the beasts remaindered from the Fall,
it was St. Chimp who rallied soonest to the cause,

a monk who followed neither order nor the law
but rocked the Ark

and drowned poor Nature, God and all.

Praise Music

Even the hyena
does not hate the gazelle

it ambushes at the waterhole.
Or virus mock the cell it withers.

The sun is not drunk with power,
nor gravity count the things that fall.

An echo does not cling to the canyon wall
or gravedigger blame the holes he must fill.

The owl's eye for the kitten is as sacred
as a cloud's aerial demotic

or the Altarpiece at Ghent.
Light, wind, blood, water, ash;

each must keep its own time.
And the mystery is not ours to praise.

Because love's true delight
is indifference —

a mockingbird
which knows nothing of night or day,

but troubles our sleep
by singing joyously,

even in the dark.

Psalm 152 (A Song of Ascent)

Dying of Parkinson's
my mother's handwriting
grew smaller.

As if determined
to erase themselves,
the words conspired
to see what late crumbs
could be shaken loose.

How at the end
her mind faltered,
           grounded
like an engineless plane
or a misbehaving child;

and lovely Lois
got mean,

the kindness stuttered
right out of her,
      a resentful tremolo,

too old and far gone
to renege on any deal,

neither continent
nor competent to choose —

the microscopic postcard
of her life
not even worth
the stamp it took
to mail it.

And mistaking me
for my dead father,
                complained
about their sex life,
the loss of her studio,
and her inability to paint —

not to mention
the ingratitude
                of her children.

And how God,
like an inattentive husband,
half-listening, had yawned
at her Fred Astaire lamentation

the way sleepers on waking
rub their eyes,
                rollover,
and go back to sleep

It was no substitute, her prayers,
for the real thing;
like an alcoholic's
                sparkling water,

it only pointed
to the greater loss.

Like my poor father, predeceased.
Glad, I'm sure,
to finally be rid of himself —
his catheter snaked
                    into the darkest corners
of his bladder,
a urological Frankenstein
                        cobbled together
from mismatched bits
of a jigsawed stomach,

haunted by the shadow of a tumor
large enough for a radiologist
to tell time by —

grateful, I'm sure,
for the whole mess
to go up in smoke
            like one of his cheap cigars.

My parents
sparred for 65 years,
familiarly and without ceasing.

Their rope-a-dope marriage
went the distance —
                a draw by any honest referee's
reckoning.

To love, I learned from them,
is to contend
                even to the bitter end.

Bookended now,
they can have their barbed colloquies
without rancor
                    and in peace.

At last a meeting of two hearts,
          two minds,

                    blended perfectly.

He in one cool corner
of their columbarium niche;

she wedged, quite comfortably,
in the other.

State of the Universe Address

Lights out
in this arm of the galaxy

where things spiral wondrously
out of control.

Stars glittering like sequins
on a party girl's miniskirt

vanilla sprinkles frosting the void
of a trillion-year old birthday cake.

And the Good Lord,
our Birthday Boy,

poised in his high chair
waiting patiently, so patiently,

to blow out the candles.

Counting Crows

When Machine Gun Kelly rolled into Oklahoma
my dad was a farm boy in Okeene. His world
was a simple venue of unlocked doors,
Wednesday evening prayer meetings, drugstore
soda fountains, and Co-op elevators.
Happiness was measured in bushels,
then meted out on high school scoreboards.

Even tonsils got yanked out on the kitchen table.

My mother, on the other hand, was from Tulsa,
a town with decidedly rougher edges.
Her father, a former law man, killed crows
with dynamite, one stick in a 55-gallon drum
packed with gravel and hung from tree roosts.
Grandpa charged 2 cents a head (when he could
find them) and traveled from farm to farm.
You could follow the trail of splintered
trees from Oklahoma to Missouri.

He enjoyed his work — especially the occasional turn
with a farmer's daughter whom he'd sport with
in the back seat of his Model T, right next to his box
of Atlas blasting caps. My grandmother and my mother
were casualties of his dynamiting career, my mother
being conceived somewhere along the back roads
of northwest Missouri after an explosion
in the rear end of his Ford.

But I digress.

It would not be easy imagining all
these lives intersecting, all these accidents
of history fleshed out then blown to bits
like crows — leaving only random pieces
to be counted like beads on an abacus.
But time gets marked different ways:
the meeting of my father and mother
at an Oklahoma State Kappa Sig mixer in 1941,
my birth ten years later, and the death of
George Francis Barnes Jr, aka "Machine
Gun Kelly" in 1954.

And then there was 1930, the year Barnes
and his wife purchased a Thompson
submachine gun at the same Missouri
hardware store from which my dynamiting grandpa
bought his blasting caps and explosives.
"I was there when they walked in." Grandpa told me once.
"They were polite. That's about all I remember —
except that she was a real looker. Later I saw
the wanted poster and realized who they were.
Next time I was in Joplin I bought me a Thompson too …
just in case I ran into them again. There was a big reward."

In 1961, when I was ten, I wrote J. Edgar Hoover
asking for his autograph (I collected autographs)
and he sent me a machine signed letter with the
admonition to always obey my parents.
For the record, I never did.
Still, J. Edgar did have an eye
for handsome hoodlums, because along with
the "autograph," he enclosed two 30's era wanted posters,
one of Charles "Pretty Boy" Floyd, and the other of
George "Machine Gun Kelly" Barnes.

Grandpa never did collect his reward,
and when he died I searched everywhere
for his Thompson, but it, like so many other things
in his life, had vanished. However, not long after,
I read an interview with Machine Gun Kelly's
old cellmate at Alcatraz — then a tour guide
with the Park Service. He said Barnes
was so mild-mannered and unassuming they called him
"Pop-Gun Kelly." But he snored so loudly, they'd have to
slap his face to rouse him. And when Kelly woke
startled from sleep, disoriented and groggy,
his cellmate reported he said the same thing.
Always the same thing.

"Where am I?"

And then rolled over and went back to sleep.

If Cowboys Were Cancer Cells

They'd be driving
a herd through town

on their way
to the railhead at Lourdes,

smashing up saloons,
whoring night and day

in the brothel of your innards,
running their cattle

up and down Main Street
through the swinging doors

of your lymph nodes.
Frightening all the decent folks,

waving their guns around,
riding roughshod

over your immune system.
Rowdy bastards

and ingrates to boot.
After everything

you've given them,
you'd think they'd let up:

the bullying,
the peace they've disturbed,

all the good women they've ruined,
the long shadows they've cast.

And your inner Yul Brynner
ready to go down

with both barrels blazing.
High Noon with a drip bag.

And a gap-toothed *bandido*
looking a lot like Eli Wallach

hamming it up,
telling you that if God

hadn't wanted you sheared,
He wouldn't have made

you sheep.

Mad Science

How far we've paddled
from *Ye Olde Tidal Pool!*

Between the shark liver oil
in *Preparation H*

and *eau de vie* of *Cnidaria*
in *Prevagen,*

we soldier on.
Life's stinging tentacles

defused,
the world's our oyster.

And fins forgotten,
we've landed on our feet.

From top to bottom,
our memories jogged,

our troubled wrinkles stilled,
we gimp gamely

into a future
where even The Heavens

declare the non-event of
our passing —

And as we make
our unhurried transition

from ashes to diamonds
or dust to eco-friendly planters,

we wave goodbye,
a final act of attrition

to commemorate our timely dispersal.
A castaway's *hallelujah!*

at the sighting
of death's black sails.

To leave a bauble
for our bubble

at the check-out counter
of this cosmic dollar store

and pennies on the dollar,
pledge our depleted atoms

at The Heavenly Pawnshop;
to be redeemed or rearranged —

whichever the hell comes first.

Cultural Heritage Map

It is Bach's B Minor Mass.

It is Pol Pot's library card.

It is the invention of painless dentistry.

It is the wreck of the *Andrea Doria*.

It is Washoe signing "Tickle me!"

It is John Wayne Gacy signing an autograph.

It is Albrecht Dürer's woodcuts.

It is a stripper named Pandora.

It is Socrates in *The Phaedo*.

It is Walmart cashiers wearing surgical gloves.

It is Thomas Mann in Hollywood.

It is Liberace in Vegas.

It is a Boy Scout merit badge.

It is the Amalekites.

It is a color illustration from *The Watchtower* of Jehovah's
    Witnesses picnicking in heaven.

It is *The Mendoza Codex* with an Aztec priest holding a heart
    in his hand.

It is *The Venus of Willendorf*.

It is Mr. Potato Head.

Job's Children

I imagine him pushing out
from his mother's body
the way a swimmer pushes off
from the side of a pool.

Never mind that at 7
he still can't swim
or was born blue,
choking on the same air
he flies through now
on his Big Wheel.

Forgive his ungainliness
and awkward flapping
when he runs,
the tiptoeing,
and blind hollering
that follows him into an elevator
or as he dives headlong
into the grass or headfirst
down a playground slide.

Overlook, please,
the inexhaustible mantras
and cartoon litanies —
meltdown words and phrases
canned in the brain's jar.
As if to say: "I am what I repeat."

He does not need to be reminded
that he is different;
that is what other children are for.
But if I try hard enough,
I can imagine him
squirming in Jesus' lap.
The Great Disruptor of Routine
come to bless the automatic child.
The odd meets God,
the child who cannot be contained,
now stuck in heaven's chimney
like a fishbone in God's throat.

One of Job's unnamed first batch,
pledged on a dare
to layaway some awful truth,
never wondering, even once,
how life could be so pitiless
or how this damaged good
could breed such peculiarity

or provoke such love.

The Prodigal

I took my *wanderjahre,*
more than I can count.

The wilderness with all its in-betweens;
the rocks and hard places,

wives, children, the desert sunsets
that never measured up.

And morning's quiet *manna*
of remorse,

the daily bread of nighttime's
loud meandering.

Where, Old Boy, were you
when I rolled the stone

of my life downhill
and followed the pillar of fire

into its three-car garage?
Called my penitentiary

a "gated community"
or wrecked my sleep

on a 2000 thread count pillow?
Who knew the sharp elbow

of your blessing
would drive me to my knees,

and in your accidental kindness,
throw me on the mercy of the world.

The History Channel

Is history doomed
to repeat itself?

Only if it's a re-run
and you missed it

the first time around.
Still, facts are facts:

ancient aliens seeded earth with
hinky DNA and covered their

tracks by levitating 15 ton
stone blocks to build the Pyramids.

Even though it already happened,
Nostradamus predicted it 9000 years later

looking in the rearview mirror
from the passenger end of a horse

ridesharing with a Knight Templar
galloping backwards through time

with the Spear of Destiny
stuck up his ass.

Weatherman

For years we've watched him age.
For years, the same channel,

the same spaghetti bowl of advancing fronts,
same patient pointing, and hurricaned hair.

All the tropical depressions
that segued into killer storms.

Or lake effect snows bearing down
on hibernating Yankees.

The explanation is always
at his fingertips.

But now with darkening clouds
gathering over the heartland of his pancreas,

the climate has changed.
His bespoke suits hang looser

and the fire in his eyes
has begun to smoke.

Like the smog drifting now
from Northern Mexico into Texas,

ash from fields burned
to raze the last harvest.

And the wind howling like Little Richard
across the Trans-Pecos,

broadcasting that there's a weatherman in Houston
who's finally decided

to do something about the weather.

A Seventy-Year-Old Father Hikes Through the East Texas Piney Woods with His Seven-Year-Old Autistic Son

The world behind the world
plays hide and seek.

The Great Squirrel rounds a tree
to tease us with his absence.

Spiral nature with its dervish tail,
a whirlwind provisioned

with our daily bread (we hope)
and half-lives gone full mad,

to inch along like slugs or snails.
The snap of leaves and branches underfoot,

this hard hearing of an old house creak,
mean nothing to the boy,

whose blankness says it all.
He knows how trees express regret;

which is to say,
they keep on growing.

So which is it?
The wind in the trees

or the platypus with his golden spur?
Jury hung, the forest is its own summation.

And in silent wandering knots,
its emptiness absolves us.

Though these trees—
and this child—could care less.

Whether in this world,
we are trespassers

or guiltless as two stalks of celery,
these woods go on.

And with all the courtliness
of an aging undertaker,

the world beyond the world just smiles
and takes our hand—

leads us deeper, deeper,
into the forest.

Tooth Fairy

My dentist is a man of faith.

The evidence is irrefutable:
the praying hands in the waiting room,

the gospel tracts in brochure racks,
and the framed photograph

of the dentist's dead mother
superimposed over the image

of a risen Jesus.
Did the Good Lord know he'd be

riding shotgun with a dead woman
in a Texas dentist's office?

I ask this question every time I wait
for the frosted glass to slide

and the receptionist to call
for my turn in the chair,

feel the bite of the drill, catch
that first whiff of burning enamel,

and imagine the numbness creeping
over God, novocained in his tomb,

as helpless as any dentist
doing a root canal

in the dark.

Ask Marilyn

*"If you're wondering
if you're dreaming;
you're dreaming."*
—Marilyn vos Savant

You are genius on *Parade*.
Even your name states the case,
as axiomatic as arithmetic or the flu.

Every Sunday the Oracle speaks.
Pythia, High Priestess of Apollo,
peddling truth to *hausfraus*

and the clueless from the temple
of stretch pants, salad shooters,
and collector's dachshund mugs.

Wisdom midwifed
in the marketplace of what passes
these days for Athens.

And though Socrates
might have a word to say
about the downside of truth-telling

or the relevance of the popular vote,
who knows whether the world's navel
passes through the lobby

of a *Day's Inn* in Cleveland
or what the odds are that visitors
from Alpha Centauri will be friendly?

The truth is as terrible as death;
if by "death" we mean
the fear of never waking.

"For who knows whether the human spirit
goes up and the spirit of animals
goes down into the earth"

Or with the Sibyl of the Sunday Supplement,
which of our questions
are even worth asking.

Estate Sale

O, they are all laid out!
The tools and housewares,

Trinkets from the cruise ship honeymoon,
Along with flotsam from the nuptial wreck.

A timing light for engines out of time,
The tune-up manual for dad's Rocket 88,

And grandma's Bible with the question marks.
The globe with all the countries wrong,

The baby pictures from 100 years ago
Of antique children who grew to nothing

More than frames to gather dust;
The serving spoon that scooped

Young peas from chipped tureens,
Furniture still creaking,

With cushions unraveled at the seams,
And the almost working typewriter.

All the evidence of life now marked "As is,"
As redoubtable as the retainer case

Belonging to the teenage son
Who hanged himself one Christmas Eve

And swallowed his retainer whole.
Marked down on this last day,

Empty, memory-free,
Yours for the taking.

A real bargain.
And now only 25 cents.

Lullaby

for DVG
1923-2013

Hands know the truth about sleeping.

There is good sleeping
And there is bad sleeping.

Bad sleeping is when you wake up
And you can't feel the hand,
But you know you can't feel it.

This condition is always accompanied
By prickling, tingling, and an unpleasant sensation.
You might call it "feeling the unfeeling."

Good sleeping, on the other hand,
Is when you wake up

And the hand does not even know
It is a hand.

Two Kinds

We delight
when animals act like people

but are appalled
when people act like people.

A kitten on a skateboard
frames sentiment perfectly,

but a fat woman in the buffet line
merits only contempt.

Perhaps kindness has more to do
with being one kind of person.

The kind of person
who is the same person all the time

and kindly views all people
as being of one kind.

Because to pay in kind
is not always kind,

and though we are taught not to confuse
the noun with the adjective,

perhaps it would be better
to throw caution to the wind

so that the noun which means
"Fundamental nature or quality"

is combined with the adjective
meaning "compassionate, considerate and loving."

The two kinds would then be one kind
and the resulting word would mean,

quite unambiguously,
a kind that is

always, everywhere, and at all times—
the same.

Singularity

Life being life,
I often think of all the friends
who opted out:
a bullet here, an overdose there,
the old car in a closed garage trick,
that lonely bridge pillar on I-45.
When you're a nail, old boy,
everything looks like a hammer.
In a lighter (or darker) mood,
I make a little joke about suicide
(i.e. "I don't call it suicide, I call it scheduling.")
or answering machines that sparkle with irony:
"Hi, this is John. I'm not here right now.
Leave a message at the sound of the tone
and I'll get back to you as soon as I'm able."
And of course, there's the Facebook page
where old friends visit on your birthday
(after having been reminded)
and catch up on you — so to speak.
All the highlights, your best hits, laid out:
your bullet points pre bullet hole.

Interests, likes, friends, achievements
(minus final achievement, of course);
these are the dreams your stuff was made of.
Karma zeroed out, your lively profile winks slyly.
Now that you are a ghost in the machine
you can have this kind of fun,
haunting people with the memory
of who you were when you were,
teasing them with your smiling face,
reminding them, tongue in virtual cheek,
that the end is nowhere near
and that you go on living
whether you like it
or not.

Class of '67

Where are they now?

Why here, of course —
in the ballroom
of a third rate country club.
But who would you recognize
without a nametag?
The girl you deflowered
behind the sewage treatment plant?
(Good Lord, you wonder,
is that white-haired biddy
still a howler?)
Or the squirrel-eating Salutatorian
living off the grid
in the Adirondacks?
And what about the full partner
at *Whinney and Glick*
who worked her way through Harvard Law
as a "cabaret" dancer in the Combat Zone?
Or the bibulous professor of literature,
his tenured liver
just weeks from retirement,
now eyeing the legs
of the urologist's fourth wife.
Is it time or a trick of perspective
that brings the change-worthy here?
Bob who became Blanche
has nothing on the shy dyslexic
(the class dunce, no less!)
whose inversions
now fetch two million a pop
and grace the walls of MOMA
with his colorful retort.
Or the yearbook *gravitas*
of the "Absent Ones,"
their report cards permanently marked,
now huddled around the dead quarterback

on the trifold Memorial Board.
Do you remember when?
Music was innocent
(more or less),
and ass over elbow,
Paradise was a slippery slope
in the plasticized backseat
of your mother's Chevelle.
Your rambunctious teen years
have come to this:
pictures of grandkids
and informative discussions
about Medicare Plan B,
the ballroom lights dimming,
the silent auction about to end.
The Wild Bunch tamed,
finally whittled down to size.
Effigies of all those accidents
that waited to happen
and somehow never did,
lifting glasses at a cash bar—

going,
going.

Gone.

Cenotaph

When I consider
the suffering

that life occasions,
I remember the stars.

How badly they must sleep
to turn continuously

in their vast beds.
The gratitude they must feel

to have given themselves
so completely—

and finally collapse
in heaven's arms.

How when their fever breaks
and the light goes out of them,

the light still reaches us;
and that what we see

is not the star itself,
but its memorial,

a luminous confession
of what is no longer there.

And while we worship the light,
the stars themselves

prefer to reverence darkness,
for whom distance is love;

and endless praise,
a canticle to emptiness.

Bandera Family Practice

In the waiting room
life decays:

a walker parked in the corner
against two wheelchairs,
four issues of *Field and Stream,*
one oxygen bottle (unattended),
the wheezing old gent
transplanted to a Danish chair,
carpet pickled green,
an oh so subtle hint of upchuck,
upchuck freighted with blackberries
finishing nicely with a lush flowering of isopropyl
and subtle undertones of pus,
The Watchtower,
another religious tract entitled: "Hell is No Joke!",
an equally monitory treatise titled: "Diabetes: the Facts,"
Highlights for Children, "Hospice Care: What You Need to Know"
(these two are separate items),
A fortyish grandmother with run-flat tits and a two-ish grandson
(no tits, no teeth, no problem),
People (the magazine),
more people (the waiting room),
Texas Highways,
my copy of the Penguin *Selected Essays of Montaigne*
page 25, Book 1, Chapter 9
"Of Liars."

"Our soul happy in the present, Cares not what lies beyond."
I love it when Montaigne quotes Horace;
almost as much as when he quotes himself:
"He who fears he shall suffer,
                                already suffers what he fears."

I have a 10:30 appointment
with Dr. Khalafy.

I have no idea where he is from
or even where he went to school.

I like him because he is sympathetic
and brown.

I like him because he never frowns
and respects the rights of malingerers.

I like him because he knows my despair of diapers
and that I occasionally leak urine.

I like him because he washes his hands
before he ever touches me.

I like him because when he says "Open Wide"
what he really means is "Allah be merciful!"

I like him because when the time comes
he will gently take my hand

and tell me
          inshallah

that everything will be all right.

A Stockyard Liturgy

For Temple Grandin

O Lord—
If history is a slaughterhouse,

May our paths always curve
And be trod without diversion.

Let no sharp angle impede our progress
Or uncertainty give us pause.

Permit us to stream freely
Down the conveyer

And grant us one final hug
Before we are stunned.

As blood flows freely
Along the path

Of least resistance,
So may the meat hook

Of inevitability
Lift us high above all butchery,

And our ending,
God willing—

Be both sudden
And humane.

To a Wife Drowned while Drinking

Praise to the river
for flowing

and your hair for knitting
a net for minnows.

Praise to the bartender
for pouring

and the silt for embracing
your lithe arms.

Praise the world
for spinning

and time
for standing still.

Praise the bridge
for crossing

and the water
for accepting you as you fell.

What shall I say, dear wife,
when we meet again?

Will you have heaving gills
or rainbowed scales?

Will your tongue
unfurl like a sail

as you race
among the dead?

What shall we say to one another
in this New World —

where you drink only water
cut with tears.

Poor reeling soul
reveling now without me,

lost to whiskied night
and a jury full of stars —

holding court,
the moon your final witness,

and the soberest judge of all.

Tulsa 1959

Above all I remember the bathroom.

They were poor and there was only one.

It smelled of Clubman and cold cream,
attar of roses and White Owl cigars.

A.L.'s razor strop hanging from a penny nail,
head hammered flat since 1925,
and on the ledge, a cow-licked shaving brush
standing bristles up. A toilet that
hawked before it up and spit.
The water splashed your crack
and tickled every time. The pipes
that strangled when the faucets ran,
howling bloody murder as they kicked
to life behind a glaze of lumpy plaster.

Below, white tile snowed with 40 years of drifting talc
and two mirrors hung to face each other.

See for yourself.

Your face, your life, affirmed in perpetuity.
You and you and you. And you again.
You the infinite regress.

You the ongoing argument
for you the ongoing argument.

And so A.L. the matter's settled:
you *do* go on forever —
at least the *front* of you.

On the night stand were their dentures;
smiling from two teacups, credit teeth
bought on time from a credit dentist
in Kansas City
"Cheap, but good chewers,"
A.L. used to say.
"He made us a deal."

Beneath the pillow his black-gripped Colt,
a loaded Peacemaker caliber .45LC,
hammer down on an empty chamber.
In his wandering days, before the War
(the Great one he'd remind you),
he'd been a trooper up in Michigan,
and had the photograph to prove it.

A.L. on a horse named Bucky, circa 1913.
State police campaign hat, brim pushed up,
Sam Brown belt, and lever action Marlin in a saddle boot.
It was the younger him, alright,
cigar in mouth, the smoking skeptic,
looking for all the world like he was bored.
Which in fact, he was.

And the creaky wooden floors
which even as a small child
held me up; those same floors
that squeaked and sagged,
we hugged so tightly in the hallway
when the twisters came.

To us there was no firmer ground.
Such lowness could drive storms away
or at the least keep us from being hoovered up

or so we thought.

My mother reading OZ by candlelight,
unshakeable and bright.
Grandma doing needlepoint.
Grandpa calmly smoking.
We children terrified,
while all around the twisters raged,
their random terror
no match for Baum or Dr. Seuss.

It must have worked
because they missed us every time.
Such mother's magic did not lift us up from Kansas
or drop us on the road to Emerald City
but took us to a stranger place.

This world was Tulsa:

the house of my grandparents
2236 East 7th street.

We are in Oklahoma.
It is 1959.

That is me in the mirror.

School of Life

For Aaron Graham

I got passing grades mostly.

The teachers were nothing
to write home about

and I spent most of class
dreaming.

I took a lot of wrong turns—
the barmaid in Galveston

with nylon seams
tattooed down her legs.

And all that time wasted
trying to close-caption the universe.

I may not have seen the light,
but I poked around

the darkness long enough
to get the message.

Does a hinge care
which way the door swings

or what the truth is
about Atlantis?

That *This Old House*
is no fixer-upper

or that the Good Lord
is to be feared

not because He's good,
but because He's sneaky?

My stumbling to bed days
may be over,

but the prayers of my youth
have never changed:

"O Lord, protect me
from waking up in strange places."

In this feast called Life,
the sins of the flesh

and the sins of the spirit
party on like Chang and Eng

on their wedding night.
Rembrandt's *Prodigal Son in the Brothel,*

lifting his glass to toast the future,
the dark colors,

the *roué's* twinkling eye,
the lap-sitting hooker on standby.

And there, under her petticoat,
the Old Master's final touch —

God's hand where it shouldn't be.

The Dead Can Swing Too

So maybe death is like a ballroom
with a hundred thousand-dollar bandstand
and a thirty-piece orchestra and the dance band
plays music from the forties and all the people dress
in their best party clothes and swing to tunes from
Benny Goodman, Glenn Miller,
Count Basie, and Artie Shaw.
Everyone whirls magically light of step
returning to their partners after every dip and turn,
and no one stumbles or trips over their own feet
or their partner's, and best of all,
when the music stops

everybody gets a chair.

ACKNOWLEDGMENTS

Grateful acknowledgment is made to the following publications in which these poems first appeared: "Magic" in *Prime Number;* "Original Sin," "Groundwork of the Metaphysics of Morals," and "The Blessing of the Animals" in *Chiron Review;* "Mockumentary" in *The Broadkill Review;* "Free Survival Guide" in *Crosswinds;* "To the Barmaid at Clifford's Bar and Grill" in *Cloudbank;* "Country Funeral" in *Cleaver;* "Visit to a Small Planet" in *Passager;* "Marriage" in *The Moth* (Ireland) and also reprinted in *The Irish Times;* "Heaven" and "For a Child Dead from a Playground Fall" in *The Galway Review* (Ireland); "At the Huguenot Cemetery" in *Soul-Lit;* "Paradise," "State of the Universe Address," and "The Dead Can Swing Too," in *SoftBlow;* "Praise Music" in *Slippery Elm;* "Psalm 152" in *The Naugatuck Review;* "Counting Crows" in *Solstice;* "If Cowboys Were Cancer Cells" in *Crab Creek Review;* "Cultural Heritage Map" in *Magnolia Review;* "The Prodigal" and "Job's Children" in *New Madrid;* "Mad Science" in *Masque and Spectacle;* "The History Channel" in *Dash;* "Tooth Fairy" and "To a Wife Drowned while Drinking" in *Blue Bonnet Review;* "Estate Sale" in *Marathon Literary Review;* "Lullaby" in *Sweet Tree;* "Two Kinds" in *Origami;* "Singularity" in *Carbon Culture;* "Cenotaph" in *Into the Void* (Ireland); "Bandera Family Practice" in *West Texas Literary Review;* "A Stockyard Liturgy" in *The Tishman Review;* and "Tulsa 1959" in *Lost Coast.*

About the Author

D.G. Geis is the author of *Fire Sale* (Tupelo Press/Leapfolio) and *Mockumentary* (Main Street Rag). Most recently, his poetry has appeared in The Irish Times, Fjords, Chiron, Skylight 47 (Ireland), A New Ulster Review (N. Ireland), Crannog Magazine (Ireland), The Moth, (Ireland), Into the Void (Ireland), Poetry Scotland (Open Mouse), The Naugatuck River Review, The Tishman Review, Zoomorphic (U.K.), The Kentucky Review, Ink and Letters, The Journal of Creative Geography, Solstice, The Worcester Review, Broad River Review, Press 53, Passager, Cloudbank, Prime Number, Soul-Lit, Crab Creek Review, Masque and Spectacle, Psaltery and Lyre, Cleaver, The New Guard, and Under the Radar (Nine Arches Press UK). He was the winner of the 2017 Firman Houghton Prize, the 2017 Emrys Prize, and was shortlisted for both the 2017 Ballymaloe International Poetry Prize (Ireland) and the 2017 Percy French Prize (Strokestown International Poetry Prize, Ireland). He was also a finalist for The New Alchemy (University of Alaska) and Fish Prizes (Ireland); and a finalist for the 2016 Main Street Rag Chapbook Competition, the 2016 Edna St. Vincent Millay Prize, the 2016 Louis Award, the 2016 Rash Award, the 2017 Prime Number Magazine Award for Poetry, the University of Memphis' Pinch Prize, and the 2017 Emrys Chapbook Prize. He divides his time between Galveston and the Hill Country of Central Texas.

Printed in September 2018
by Gauvin Press,
Gatineau, Québec